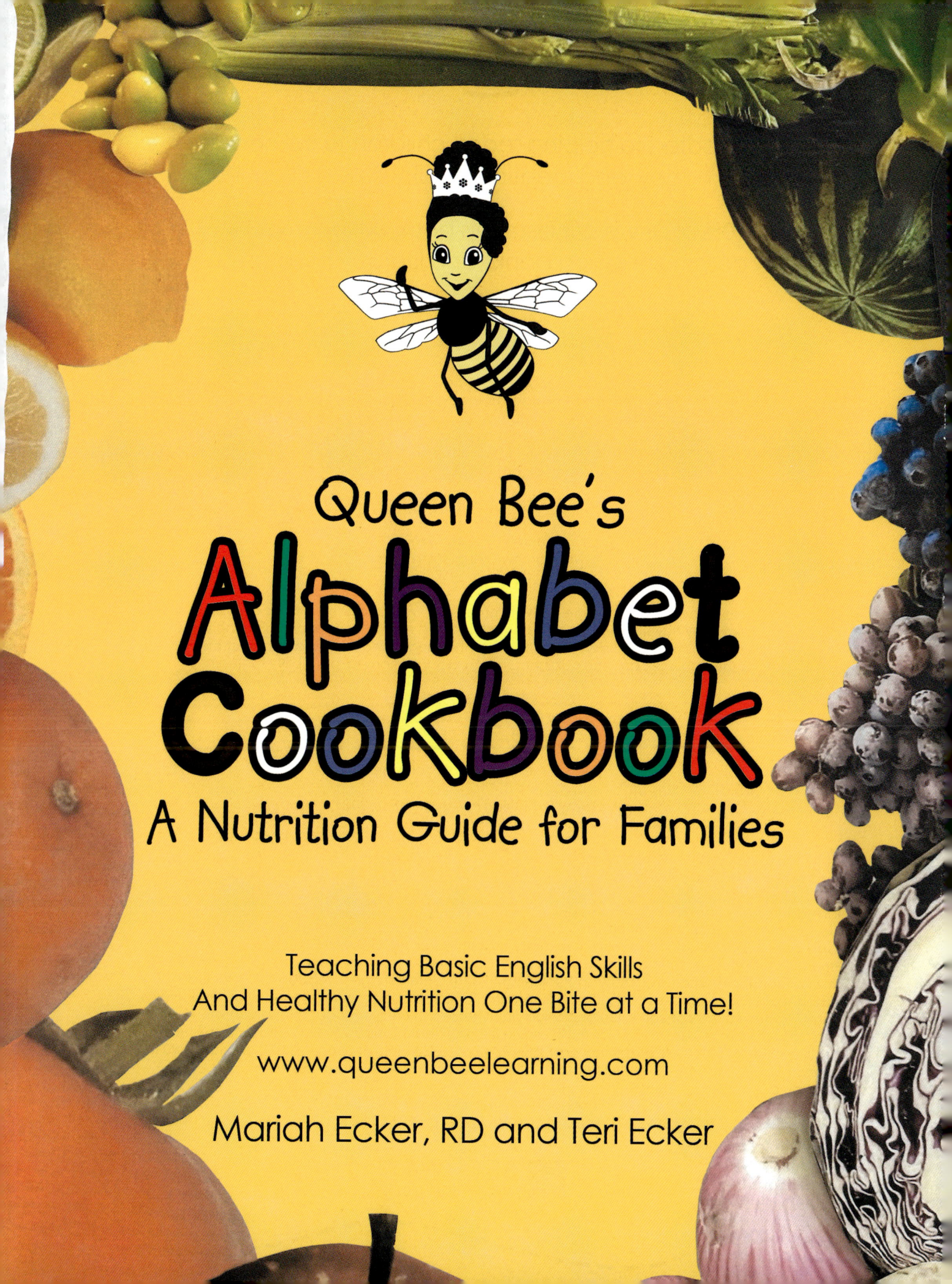

Dedicated to helping teach children to be healthy and happy, and creating quality time for families.

10% of any profit from this book will be given to community food banks and literacy programs.

Copyright © 2021 Mariah Ecker, RD and Teri Ecker.

All rights reserved. No part of this book may be used or reproduced by any means, graphic, electronic, or mechanical, including photocopying, recording, taping or by any information storage retrieval system without the written permission of the author except in the case of brief quotations embodied in critical articles and reviews.

Archway Publishing books may be ordered through booksellers or by contacting:

Archway Publishing
1663 Liberty Drive
Bloomington, IN 47403
www.archwaypublishing.com
844-669-3957

Because of the dynamic nature of the Internet, any web addresses or links contained in this book may have changed since publication and may no longer be valid. The views expressed in this work are solely those of the author and do not necessarily reflect the views of the publisher, and the publisher hereby disclaims any responsibility for them.

ISBN: 978-1-6657-0890-6 (sc)
ISBN: 978-1-6657-0888-3 (hc)
ISBN: 978-1-6657-0889-0 (e)

Printed in the United States of America.

Archway Publishing rev. date: 10/13/2021

Publisher's Cataloging-In-Publication Data
(Prepared by The Donohue Group, Inc.)

Names: Ecker, Mariah, author. | Ecker, Teri, author.
Title: Queen Bee's alphabet cookbook : a nutrition guide for families : teaching basic English skills and healthy nutrition one bite at a time! / Mariah Ecker, RD, and Teri Ecker.
Other Titles: Alphabet cookbook
Description: Bloomington, IN : Archway Publishing, [2021] | Interest age level: 001-009. | Include bibliographical references and index. | Summary: "Children's book to help teach early English skills, and healthy eating concepts. Guides loving adult helpers in creating educational activities for children of various ages and helps them create lifelong healthy eaters"-- Provided by publisher.
Identifiers: ISBN 9781665708906 (softcover) | ISBN 9781665708883 (hardcover) | ISBN 9781665708890 (ebook)
Subjects: LCSH: Nutrition--Juvenile literature. | English language--Alphabet--Juvenile literature. | Cooking--Juvenile literature. | CYAC: Nutrition. | English language--Alphabet. | Cooking. | LCGFT: Cookbooks. | Alphabet books.
Classification: LCC RA784 .E35 2021 (print) | LCC RA784 (ebook) | DDC 613.2--dc23

CONTENTS

SEEDS: Planting seeds of curiosity and knowledge

The Alphabet 1

SPROUTS: Watching new talents and ideas emerge

Table Setting Illustration 29
100 Words 30
Kitchen and Cooking Safety Rules 33
Learning Nutrition: Balanced Plate 35
A Few Herbs and Seasonings to Learn 37
Cooking Measurements 38
Good Activities for Little Chefs 39
10 Easy Recipes to do with an Adult Helper 40

SEEDLINGS: Growing new skills and sharing the fun of learning

40 Fun Recipes for the Growing Chef 53
How to Make a Smoothie 87
Tips on First Foods for Babies 95
Growing Lifelong Healthy Eaters 97
Ways of Using the Alphabet Cookbook, and your Imagination as a Learning Tool for all Ages! 101
References 103

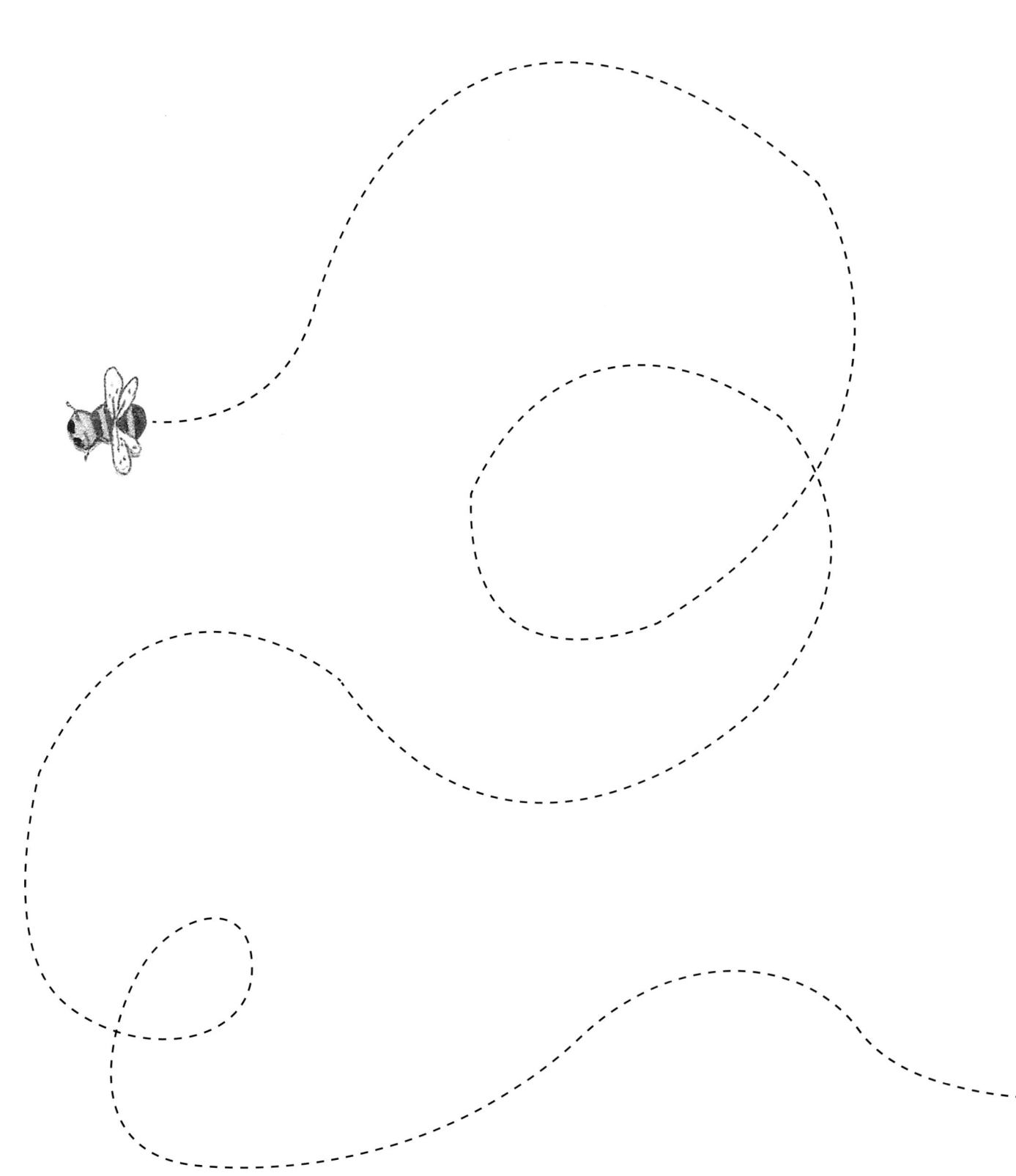

SEEDS: Planting seeds of curiosity and knowledge

A is for apple.
It grows on a tree.
For apples to grow
on the trees we need bees.

B is for bread
and butter and baking.
All of the wonderful
things we'll be making.

C is for carrot and cookies and cake.
So many good things to learn how to make.

D is for dinner, delicious to eat.
Go to the table and pull up a seat.

E is for egg.
It comes from a chicken
With eggs you can
cook food that is
'finger licking'.

G is for garden,
where vegetables grow,
on bushes or vines
or planted in rows.

H is for honey,
the bees make it sweet.
Things made with honey
are so good to eat.

I is for ice cream,
a frozen treat.
Eat on a hot day
to beat the heat!

J is for jam,
and also for jelly.
These are so good
you will say "get in my belly!"

K is for kitchen.
The room where we cook,
making the recipes
from our cookbook!

L is for lemon,
and also for lime.
They taste a bit sour
most of the time.

M is for milk.
From cows, nuts or soy.
It tastes so good
you will jump with joy!

N is for nut.
Nuts make a good snack.
Cashews or almonds
can go in a sack.

O is for orange,
the color and fruit.
Would you like to wear
a fancy orange suit?

P is for peanut,
and peanut butter spread.
Nothing is better
with jelly on bread.

R is for raisins.
So naturally sweet.
Who knew dried grapes
could make a great treat?

S is for smoothie,
a healthy drink.
Pick your fruits and veggies,
and wash them in the sink.

T is for tomato.
Red, round and sweet.
In sauces and salads,
so yummy to eat!

V is for vegetables.
So good for you.
Eat them each day,
your body thanks you.

W is for watermelon.
A sweet summer snack.
Green skin with red fruit,
and seeds that are black.

X is for the extra special way it makes you feel, when helping in the kitchen to make delicious meals.

Y is for yellow.
Pineapple for lunch,
or a banana,
picked from a bunch.

Z is for Zucchini,
Yellow or green.
Both are good and
in the garden are seen.

SPROUTS: Watching new talents and ideas emerge

1. Plate
2. Placemat
3. Fork
4. Napkin
5. Bowl
6. Cup
7. Spoon
8. Knife
9. Table
10. Chair

100 WORDS

1. Almond
2. Alphabet
3. Apple
4. Avocado
5. Baking
6. Banana
7. Bee
8. Belly
9. Black
10. Blue
11. Body
12. Bowl
13. Bread
14. Breakfast
15. Brown
16. Cake
17. Carrot
18. Cashew
19. Chair
20. Chicken

21. Chop
22. Cook
23. Cookbook
24. Cookie
25. Cup
26. Delicious
27. Dessert
28. Dinner
29. Drink
30. Eat
31. Egg
32. Farm
33. Farmer
34. First
35. Foil
36. Food
37. Fork
38. Fruit
39. Garden
40. Good
41. Grape
42. Green
43. Grow
44. Healthy
45. Honey
46. Ice
47. Ice Cream
48. Jam
49. Jelly
50. Juice
51. Kitchen
52. Knife
53. Last
54. Lemon
55. Lettuce
56. Letter
57. Lime
58. Lunch
59. Measure
60. Mix

61. Milk
62. Napkin
63. Nut
64. Orange
65. Oven
66. Pan
67. Peanut
68. Peanut Butter
69. Pepper
70. Plate
71. Purple
72. Queen
73. Raisin
74. Recipe
75. Red
76. Salad
77. Salad Dressing
78. Salsa
79. Salt
80. Sea
81. Snack
82. Sour
83. Spoon
84. Spread
85. Sprinkle
86. Stir
87. Stovetop
88. Sweet
89. Table
90. Tablespoon
91. Tart
92. Taste
93. Teaspoon
94. Tomato
95. Up
96. Vegetable
97. Watermelon
98. White
99. Yellow
100. Zucchini

KITCHEN AND COOKING SAFETY RULES

KITCHEN RULES:

Make sure there is a fire extinguisher and everyone knows where it is. There should also be first aid supplies available.

Make sure the cooking area is prepped for safety by securing any loose cords, putting knives out of reach and a child safety lock on the drawers with sharp objects. Cleaning supplies, alcoholic beverages, plastic wrap, and any other potentially dangerous items moved away.

Make sure everyone has long hair tied back, sleeves rolled up, no loose or dangling clothes or jewelry to get in the way. Non slip shoes are good in the kitchen too. Get your child their own special apron to help keep their clothes clean.

With young children prep the items in advance so you can pay attention to them and not be distracted.

Make sure everyone washes their hands, under their fingernails and up to their elbows before beginning.

Keep any electrical appliances away from water to avoid shocks. Stay away from plugs and sockets if your hands are wet.

Clean your counters you will be using before you start.

Rinse your fruits and vegetables in the sink before using.

Use separate cutting boards for meats than fruits or vegetables.

Always cook meat to the correct temperature.

Keep food out of the temperature danger zone: 40-140 degrees F. Refrigerate leftovers right away.

Do not put cooked meat back on any surface that had raw meat on it. Always use a clean plate. Wash your hands after touching raw meat before touching other ingredients.

Clean up as you go, wiping up spills, putting used utensils in the sink and putting away knives right after use. This teaches children good habits.

Use a clean fork or spoon to taste your creations once! No double dipping or using your fingers!

KNIFE RULES:

Only adults get to get out and carry knives. Ideally children will use safety knives made for them.

Adults must supervise all knife work, cutting or chopping.

Do not put knives in a sink full of water, people might not see it and get cut.

STOVETOP AND OVEN RULES:

No touching the microwave oven, regular oven or stovetop without an adult supervising.

Watch out for hot foods, pans, lids or anything that has been in or on an oven or stovetop and could be hot! Don't touch until an adult says it is OK.

Always turn your handles of pots or pans inwards or towards the back of the stovetop to avoid accidents or burns.

Don't add water to a pan with hot oil. It will make the oil splatter and could burn someone.

Keep paper towels, dish towels and pot holders away from the stovetop to avoid fires.

Never put water on a cooking fire! It could make it bigger! Ask an adult to help put it out and use a fire extinguisher. A small fire can be put out with baking soda or smothered with a lid to the pot or pan. Leave the house and call for help if these things don't work.

If you get a burn, tell an adult immediately and hold the burn under cool running water.

Check the oven and all other cooking appliances to make sure they are turned off before you leave the kitchen.

LEARNING NUTRITION: BALANCED PLATE

Energy Foods: are carbohydrates such as rice, sweet potato, pasta, and bread. They give us the long-lasting energy we need every day to do the things we love.

Muscle Foods: are protein and come from both plants and animals. Some healthy examples are eggs, dairy, lean meats like chicken, fish, and beans. They are the building blocks to our muscles and help us grow stronger every day.

Water or Milk: Drink 6 to 8 cups of water each day! If having non-dairy milk, choose a fortified option with calcium, vitamin D, and vitamin B12 to keep your body strong and healthy.

Thinking Foods: are healthy fats such as from oils, avocado, and coconut. Not only do they make your food taste delicious and keep you full, but they help your brain to work well and your heart to stay healthy.

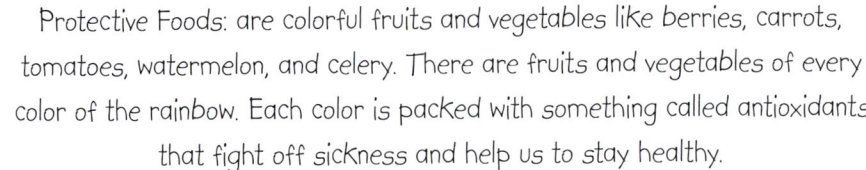

Protective Foods: are colorful fruits and vegetables like berries, carrots, tomatoes, watermelon, and celery. There are fruits and vegetables of every color of the rainbow. Each color is packed with something called antioxidants that fight off sickness and help us to stay healthy.

Sometimes Foods: treat foods are yummy to have on occasion! Make sure you are eating your other food groups too. Treat foods don't have the same benefits in helping you grow strong like the other foods do.

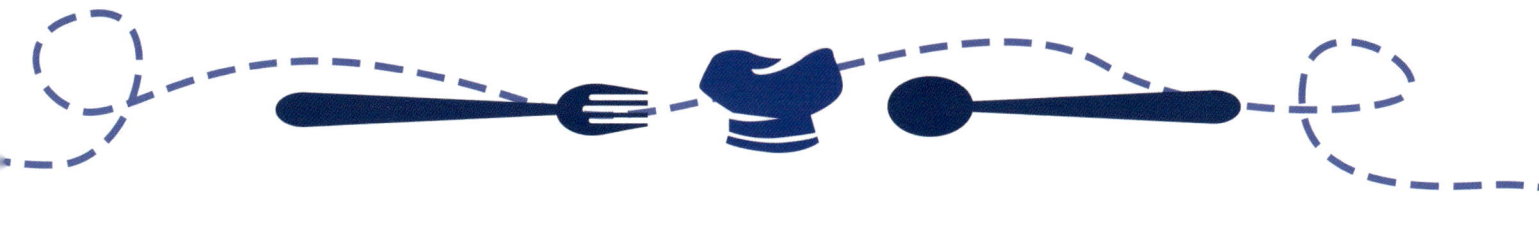

TIPS FOR PARENTS

The plate method is a healthy way to eat for the whole family! It's important to eat by example. Know that your young child will likely not eat foods in these ratios, and that is okay. Use this plate method as a reminder to try to offer foods from each food group at every meal to build familiarity.

Combining multiple food groups at meals and snacks helps both kids and adults to feel satiated by having a slow release of blood sugar which equals long-lasting energy! Use this plate as a tool to planning snacks: aim to include a protein and/or fat source at all snacks to help tide everyone over until their next meal. Fruits and vegetables will provide fiber, also helping us to feel full for longer.

There is no "perfect" fruit or vegetable that provides 100% of the vitamins and minerals needed for children or adults. Having a variety is key! Set a goal to try to eat fruits and vegetables of all colors of the rainbow each week. Each color has its own unique phytonutrients – antioxidants that have disease preventing and fighting benefits in our bodies!

A FEW HERBS AND SEASONINGS TO LEARN

A pinch of salt brings the flavor out in foods. It comes from the ocean.

Basil can be green or purple. It tastes great on Italian food like pasta and pizza.

Pepper adds a kick of spice. It comes from little pepper corn kernels that grow on a vine.

A sprig of mint is refreshing in water, tea, and desserts.

Cinnamon makes anything sweet taste like a treat. It comes from the bark of a tree.

Cilantro is a soft green herb that is yummy to use in Mexican and Asian food.

COOKING MEASUREMENTS

1 tablespoon (T) = 3 teaspoons (t)
2 tablespoons = 1 ounce (oz)
4 tablespoons = ¼ cup
8 tablespoons = ½ cup
1 cup = 8 fluid ounces
2 cups = 1 pint (pt.)
2 pints = 1 quart (qt)
2 quarts = ½ gallon (gal)
4 quarts = 1 gallon

Volume

1 fluid ounce = 30 milliliters (ml)
1 cup = 237 ml
1 pint = .47 Liter (L)
1 quart = .95 L
1 gallon = 3.79 Liters

Weight

1 ounce = 28.35 grams (g)
1 pound (lb.) = 453.6 grams
1 kilogram (kg) = 2.205 lbs.
1 lb. = 16 ounces

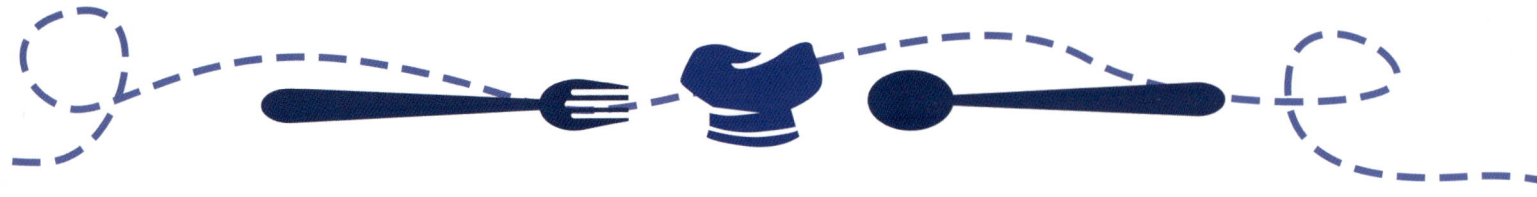

GOOD ACTIVITIES FOR LITTLE CHEFS

2-3 YEAR OLDS

Rinsing fruits and vegetables

Squeezing citrus fruits

Picking fresh herbs off of stems

Tearing herbs and green leafy vegetables

Sprinkling seasoning

Whisking and stirring

Mashing soft ingredients

Kneading dough

4-6 YEAR OLDS

Grating cheese

Breaking eggs

Using a rolling pin for dough

Using cookie cutters

Chopping with a kid safe knife

Snipping herbs with a pair of scissors

Peeling vegetables

Greasing pans

Forming patties, meatballs, and cookies

Decorating food

7-9 YEAR OLDS

Measuring dry ingredients

Helping set the table

Skewering kabobs

Scooping batter into pans and muffin cups

Using a can opener

10 YEAR OLDS AND UP

This age group is usually ready to cook independently! Make sure they are competent with following basic kitchen safety rules such as using knives safely, tucking pan handles, turning off kitchen appliances, etc. An adult should still be present in the household in case of emergency.

10 EASY RECIPES TO DO WITH AN ADULT HELPER

1) A IS FOR APPLE CRUMBLE
2) EGG MUFFINS
3) BANANA FRENCH TOAST
4) VERY BERRY JAM
5) APPLE GRILLED CHEESE
6) ANTS ON A LOG
7) COOKIE DOUGH POWER BALLS
8) FROYO BITES
9) VEGGIE PIZZA FACES
10) SUPER SALADS

A IS FOR APPLE CRUMBLE

Prep Time: 5 minutes

Cook Time: 25 minutes

Makes: 5 servings

INGREDIENTS:

3 granny smith or other tart green apples, cut into 2-inch squares

1/2 cup old-fashioned oats

1/3 cup whole-wheat flour (can substitute all-purpose or gluten free flour if desired)

1/4 cup brown sugar

1/4 cup vegetable oil such as avocado oil or coconut oil

1 tsp cinnamon

1 tsp lemon juice

DIRECTIONS:

Adults: Preheat oven to 375 F.
Together: Chop apples (peeling skin is optional).
Kids: Grease an 8x8 inch glass baking dish (for thin crumble) or a glass bread baking dish (for a thicker crumble). Add apples to bottom of the dish.
Kids: In a large bowl, mix oats, sugar, flour, cinnamon, lemon, and oil. Sprinkle this topping over the apples.
Together: Bake for 25 minutes. Remove from oven and enjoy with a scoop of vanilla ice cream!

EGG MUFFINS

Prep Time: 0 minutes

Cook Time: 15-20 minutes

Makes: 12 muffins

INGREDIENTS:
5 eggs

¼ cup all-purpose flour (substitute cornmeal or gluten-free flour if desired)

2 Tbsp milk of choice

1 cup of fun fillings (such as zucchini, broccoli, red bell pepper for vegetables; chicken sausage, bacon, or tofu for extra protein; or even rice or quinoa)

½ cup grated cheese (mozzarella, cheddar, jack, and parmesan all work well)

Salt and pepper to taste

DIRECTIONS:

Adults: Preheat oven to 375 F.
Kids: Grease a mini muffin pan with oil.
Together: In a large bowl, lightly whisk your eggs, milk, and salt and pepper.
Together: Chop the vegetables. Add fillings, flour, and cheese to the bowl.
Kids: Mix well! Fill each muffin cup all the way up with batter.
Adults: Bake for 15-20 minutes, or until firm to touch and turning golden brown at edges.

BANANA FRENCH TOAST

Prep Time:
5 minutes

Cook Time:
10 minutes

Makes:
4 pieces

INGREDIENTS:
1 ripe banana

1 egg

4 slices bread (whatever you have on hand)

1 tsp cinnamon

Butter or vegetable oil for cooking

DIRECTIONS:

Kids: Peel and mash the banana in a medium bowl, and then whisk in then egg. Add the cinnamon and whisk well.

Kids: Take 1 piece of bread and put into the banana egg mixture. Let it sit in the mixture for 1-2 minutes, making sure both sides of bread are coated.

Together: Heat a small knob of oil or butter in a pan. Cook each side of the bread for 1-2 minutes or until golden brown.

Together: Cut into fun shapes like triangles or strips and serve.

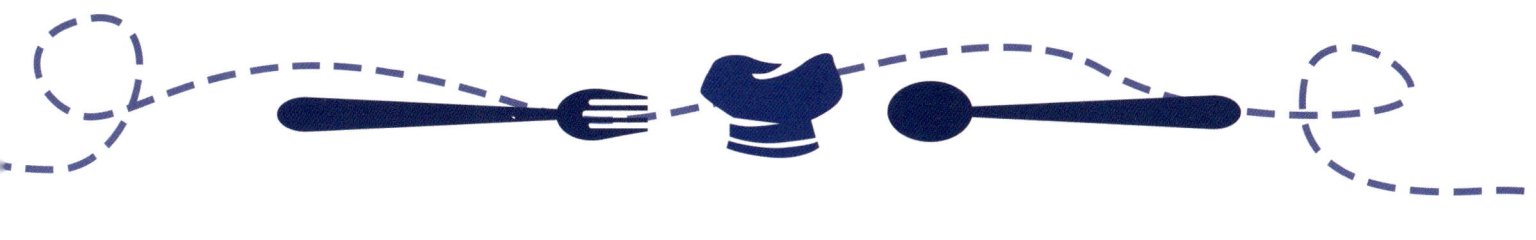

VERY BERRY JAM

Prep Time: 5 minutes

Refrigerator time: 1 hour

Makes: 1 cup

INGREDIENTS:
2 cups of your favorite berries (such as strawberries, blueberries, raspberries, or blackberries)
4 Tbsp chia seeds
2 Tbsp honey*
1/2 tsp vanilla extract

DIRECTIONS:
Together: Blend berries in a blender or mash with a fork.
Kids: Add the chia seeds and vanilla extract. Stir until mixed. Spoon into a container and let it set in the refrigerator for 1 hour.
*Don't serve honey to children under 1 year old due to risk of infant botulism

APPLE GRILLED CHEESE

Prep Time: 5 minutes

Cook Time: 10 minutes

Makes: 2 sandwiches

INGREDIENTS:

4 slices of your favorite sandwich bread

4 slices of your favorite cheese (such as cheddar, jack, or mozzarella)

1 granny smith apple, sliced

1 Tbsp butter

DIRECTIONS:

Kids: Place the sandwich bread on a flat surface. Spread butter on one side of each piece of bread.

Together: Slice the apples and cheese.

Kids: Assemble the sandwiches. Make sure the buttered sides are on the outside. Fill the inside with 2 cheese slices and apple.

Together: Heat a medium sized non-stick skillet over medium-high heat. Grill the sandwiches for about 3 minutes on each side or until bread is golden and cheese is melted. Serve while warm!

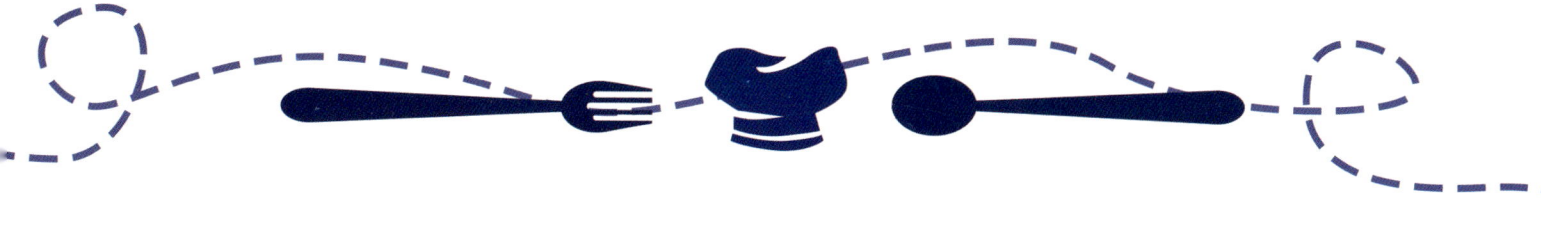

ANTS ON A LOG

Prep Time: 5 minutes

Makes: 2 servings

INGREDIENTS:

2 celery stalks

Peanut butter (or other spreads like almond or sunflower butter, cream cheese, or guacamole)

Raisins (or other fun toppings like cranberries, fresh berries, pretzels, and peas)

DIRECTIONS:

Together: Cut the celery stalks in 2 or 3 pieces

Kids: Spread peanut butter or other dip on the celery. Top with raisins or other fun choices!

COOKIE DOUGH POWER BALLS

Prep Time: 10 minutes

Cook Time: 25 minutes

Makes: 20 balls

INGREDIENTS:

1 cup creamy peanut butter (non-hydrogenated)

¼ cup pure maple syrup

1 ½ cups rolled oats

½ cup semi-sweet chocolate chips

DIRECTIONS:

Together: Stir peanut butter and maple syrup in a bowl. Add the oats and chocolate chips. Mix well.

Kids: Roll the dough into balls. Try on one if you'd like, and then refrigerate the rest to have a power ball snack later!

FRO-YO BITES

Prep Time: 5 minutes

Chill Time: 4-6 hours

Makes: 1 silicone tray

INGREDIENTS:
1 cup whole milk vanilla Greek yogurt
½ cup fresh berries, banana, or other fruit

DIRECTIONS:
Kids: Place fruit in a medium bowl and mash with a fork. Add yogurt and stir.
Kids: Spoon the mixture into a silicone mold tray.
Together: Place the mold into your freezer and freeze for 4-6 hours.
Together: Pop fro-yo bites from the mold and enjoy!

VEGGIE PIZZA FACES

Prep Time: 15 minutes

Cook Time: 15 minutes

Makes: 2 servings

INGREDIENTS:

Pick your crust (enough for two people): pita bread, English muffins, tortillas, store bought or homemade pizza crust

½ cup marinara or pizza sauce

½ cup grated mozzarella cheese

1 cup of toppings: bell pepper cut into strips (for hair or mouth), olives and zucchini slices (for eyes), broccoli (for eyebrows), cherry tomatoes or carrots (for nose), fresh basil (for mustache or hair), and many more using your imagination!

DIRECTIONS:

Adults: Preheat oven to 400 F.

Together: Spread each crust with sauce and sprinkle cheese on top. Arrange vegetables to make funny faces. Place on a baking sheet and bake for 10-15 minutes, or until vegetables are soft and cheese is melted. Take pictures and enjoy!

SUPER SALADS

Prep Time: 10-20 minutes

Makes: As much as you want

Salads aren't just green. They can be made with your favorite fruits, veggies, noodles and grains, nuts, and cheese. Get creative with your own super salad!

INGREDIENTS:

Using the picture of food groups on page 35, pick 1-2 ingredients from each group to make a salad. Some of our favorite combinations are:

- Pasta salad: pasta noodles, peas, tomato, and mozzarella cheese
- Taco salad: shredded lettuce, grated or roasted carrots, shredded cheese, and a protein like beans, shrimp, or shredded chicken
- Fruit & grain salad: brown rice or quinoa, your favorite fruits, raisins, and crushed nuts

Your favorite salad dressing. See page 58 for ideas

DIRECTIONS:

Kids: Pick your ingredients.
Together: Chop ingredients into bite size pieces. Mix together in a bowl, jar, or serve them deconstructed on a plate. Pour dressing on top or serve dressing as a dip that you can dunk your ingredients into.

SEEDLINGS: Growing new skills and sharing the fun of learning

40 FUN RECIPES FOR THE GROWING CHEF

SOUPS, DRESSINGS, SALSAS, & BREADS

SOUPS

Alphabet soup

Zoodle soup

Apple Squash soup

Enchilada soup

DRESSINGS & SALSAS

Honey orange dressing

Blueberry dressing

Ranch dressing

Honey mustard dressing

Pineapple salsa

Tasty tomato salsa

Creamy avocado sauce

BREADS & CRACKERS

Cornbread

Bakery bread

Cheesy crackers

MEALS

Butternut squash mac and cheese

Classic mac and cheese

Family style rainbow tacos

Egg roll bowl

Baked chicken (or tofu) tenders

Melty quesadillas with spinach

Simple peanut noodles

Spaghetti squash alfredo

Veggie taquitos

Hawaiian fried rice

Peanut butter curry

Lemon butter pasta

DESSERTS

Coconut sweet rice with mango

Chocolate pudding

Frozen banana pops

Rainbow fruit kabobs with healthy cake batter dip

Watermelon popsicles

Carrot cake cookies

DRINKS

Electrolyte buzz

So berry delicious sun tea

Horchata

Hot cocoa

How to make a smoothie

Orange sunrise smoothie

Chocolate monkey smoothie

Very vanilla smoothie

Strawberry cake shake

SOUPS
ALPHABET SOUP

Prep Time: 15 minutes

Cook Time: 30 minutes

Makes: 6 servings

INGREDIENTS:
2 Tbsp butter or vegetable oil such as olive, avocado, or coconut oil
1 medium onion
2 carrots (peeling is optional)
1 sweet potato (peeling is optional)
1 cup cauliflower florets
½ cup frozen green peas
4 cups low sodium chicken or vegetable broth
1 – 14 ounce can diced tomatoes with the juice
½ cup alphabet pasta (or other available small shaped pasta)
Salt and pepper to taste

DIRECTIONS:
1) Prep your ingredients. Chop the onion, carrots, sweet potato, and cauliflower.
2) Heat the butter or oil in a large soup pot over medium heat. Add the vegetables to the pot. Stir often for about 5 minutes or until the vegetables begin to soften.
3) Add the broth and diced tomatoes. Bring to a boil, then turn down heat and simmer for 20 minutes until everything is soft.
4) Add the pasta and peas. Cook for another 5 minutes.
5) Season with salt and pepper to taste.

ZOODLE SOUP

Prep Time: 15 minutes

Cook Time: 20 minutes

Makes: 6 servings

INGREDIENTS:
1 pound boneless and skinless chicken breasts, cut into 1-inch cubes (can sub firm tofu)
2 Tbsp vegetable oil such as olive, avocado, or coconut oil
1 medium onion
2 stalks celery
2 carrots (peeling is optional)
4 cups of low sodium chicken or vegetable broth
1 bay leaf
3 zucchinis for "zoodles"
2 Tbsp lemon juice
Salt and pepper to taste
Fresh parsley to top

DIRECTIONS:
1) Prep ingredients. Cube chicken and on a separate cutting board dice the onion, celery, and carrots. Make your zucchini noodles by using a spiralizer or a julienne peeler
2) Heat 1 Tbsp oil in large soup pot over medium heat. Add cubed chicken (or tofu) and cook for 3 minutes or until golden on outside.
3) Turn down heat to low-medium. Add remaining 1 Tbsp of oil, onion, celery, and carrots. Stir often for 3-5 minutes until onions are translucent and vegetables are soft.
4) Add broth and bay leaf. Bring to a boil and then reduce heat. Add your zoodles and cook for 3-5 minutes.
5) Season with lemon juice, salt and pepper to taste, and top with fresh parsley.

APPLE SQUASH SOUP

Prep Time:
15 minutes

Cook Time:
30 minutes

Makes:
6 servings

INGREDIENTS:
1 Tbsp butter or vegetable oil such as olive, avocado, or coconut oil
1 medium butternut squash (peeling is optional)
1 medium onion
2 stalks celery
1 medium apple (tart apples work well, such as granny smith)
4 cups low sodium chicken or vegetable broth
Salt and pepper to taste

DIRECTIONS:
1) Prep your ingredients. Chop the butternut squash, onion, celery, and apple.
2) Heat the butter or oil in a large soup pot over medium heat. Add the squash, onion, celery, and apple to the pot. Stir often for about 10 minutes to allow the squash to begin to soften.
3) Add broth and bring to a boil, then turn down heat and allow to simmer for 20 minutes until everything is soft.
4) Puree soup using a blender by filling blender halfway up at a time. Season with salt and pepper to taste.

ENCHILADA SOUP

Prep Time: 15 minutes

Cook Time: 20 minutes

Makes: 6 servings

INGREDIENTS:

2 Tbsp vegetable oil such as olive, avocado, or coconut oil
1 medium onion
2 garlic cloves
3 Tbsp chili powder
1 tsp cumin
½ tsp smoked paprika
4 cups low sodium chicken or vegetable broth
2 – 15-ounce cans of black or pinto beans
1 cup of corn (fresh or frozen)
1 – 28 ounce can of fire-roasted crushed tomatoes
Juice of ½ lime
Salt and pepper to taste
Optional toppings: shredded cheese, sour cream or Greek yogurt, tasty tomato salsa, avocado, green onions, olives, fresh cilantro

DIRECTIONS:

1) Prep your ingredients. Chop the onion and mince garlic. Drain and rinse your beans.
2) Heat the oil in a large soup pot over medium heat. Add the onion and garlic to the pot. Stir often for 3-5 minutes until onions are translucent.
3) Add the chili powder, cumin, paprika, broth, crushed tomatoes, beans and corn. Bring to a boil, then turn down heat and simmer for 20 minutes until everything is soft.
4) Season with lime juice, salt and pepper to taste. Serve with your favorite toppings.

DRESSINGS & SALSAS
SALAD DRESSINGS – 4 WAYS

Prep Time: 5 minutes

Makes: about 1 cup dressing

DIRECTIONS:
1) For the Orange Honey, Ranch, and Honey Mustard Dressings: measure ingredients into a bowl or large jar. Stir well with a fork or whisk.
2) For the Blueberry dressing: measure ingredients into a blender. Blend on low until blueberries are broken down.

ORANGE HONEY DRESSING

INGREDIENTS:
½ cup olive oil
Juice of ½ medium orange
Juice of ½ lemon
2 tsp honey
Pinch salt to taste

RANCH DRESSING

INGREDIENTS:
1 cup Greek yogurt
2 tsp apple cider vinegar
1/2 tsp garlic powder
1/2 tsp onion powder
1/2 tsp dried dill
Salt and pepper to taste

BLUEBERRY DRESSING

INGREDIENTS:
½ cup blueberries, fresh or frozen
¼ cup vinegar (white or apple cider)
¼ cup honey
1/3 cup olive oil
Pinch salt to taste

HONEY MUSTARD DRESSING

INGREDIENTS:
¼ cup Dijon mustard
¼ cup honey
¼ cup apple cider vinegar
¼ cup olive oil
1 Tbsp lemon juice
Salt and pepper to taste

SALSA – 2 Ways

Prep Time: 10 minutes

Makes: 4 servings

DIRECTIONS:
1) Dice and chop your ingredients. Try using scissors to cut the cilantro.
2) In a medium bowl, mix everything together well. Season with salt and pepper to taste.
3) Serve with tortilla chips, on tacos, or salads!

PINEAPPLE SALSA

INGREDIENTS:
1 cup pineapple
2 medium tomatoes
¼ cup red onion
1 Tbsp green bell pepper (or jalapeno)
¼ cup cilantro
Juice of 1 lime
Salt and pepper to taste

TASTY TOMATO SALSA

INGREDIENTS:
2 medium tomatoes
2 Tbsp green bell pepper (or jalapeno)
1 garlic clove
1 Tbsp cilantro
Juice of ½ lime
Salt and pepper to taste

CREAMY AVOCADO SAUCE

Prep Time: 10 minutes

Makes: 4 servings

INGREDIENTS:
2 avocados
1 cup Greek yogurt
Juice of 1 lime
1 clove garlic
1 jalapeno with seeds removed (optional to leave some for spice)
¼ cup cilantro
¼ cup water
Salt and pepper to taste

DIRECTIONS:
1) Add all ingredients to a blender and blend until creamy with no chunks
2) Serve with tortilla chips, on tacos, or salads!

BREADS & CRACKERS
CORNBREAD

Prep Time: 10 minutes

Cook Time: 25 minutes

Makes: 8 servings

INGREDIENTS:
1 cup all-purpose flour (can sub whole wheat or gluten-free alternative)
1 cup cornmeal
¼ cup sugar
1 Tbsp baking powder
½ tsp salt
2 eggs (can sub 2 flax eggs for a vegan alternative: 2 Tbsp ground flax seeds mixed in 6 Tbsp water)
1/3 cup butter or coconut oil, melted
1 ¼ cup milk of choice (can sub any non-dairy milk)

DIRECTIONS:
1) Preheat oven to 375 F. Grease a square glass baking dish or cast-iron skillet.
2) In a medium bowl, mix dry ingredients together: flour, cornmeal, sugar, salt, and baking powder.
3) In a separate bowl, whisk together the eggs (or flax eggs), coconut oil or butter, and milk.
4) Add the wet ingredients to the dry and mix just until combined. You want the batter to be a little lumpy! Let batter sit and rest for 10 minutes.
5) Pour batter into pan or skillet and bake for 20-25 minutes, or until a fork comes out clean. Let cool before serving.

BAKERY BREAD

Prep Time: 15 minutes
Rest Time: 10 hours
Cook Time: 1 hour 15 min
Makes: 1 loaf

INGREDIENTS:

*You will need an oven safe pot (Dutch oven) for this recipe
3 cups flour (mixture of half white flour and half whole-wheat flour)
½ tsp dry active yeast
1 ½ tsp salt
1 ½ cups lukewarm water

DIRECTIONS:

1) Measure flour, yeast, and salt into a medium bowl. Mix well.
2) Add the lukewarm water. Stir well until everything is combined and smooth.
3) Cover the bowl with saran wrap and let rest for 8-10 hours on the counter.
4) Once your dough has rested, flour a surface. Move dough from bowl to floured surface, wet hands, and form dough into a ball. You do not have to knead the dough. Cover again with saran wrap and let rise for another hour.
5) While dough is rising, preheat oven to 450 F. When preheated, place Dutch oven pot into oven for 30 minutes.
6) After your dough has risen for an hour, take hot pot out of oven and place dough ball inside. Bake for 30 minutes with lid on. Then take lid off and bake for an additional 10-15 minutes.
7) Let cool before eating!

CHEESY CRACKERS

Prep Time: 15 minutes

Cook Time: 12-15 minutes

Makes: 2 dozen crackers

INGREDIENTS:
¾ cup whole-wheat flour (or can substitute a gluten-free flour if desired)
½ cup rolled oats
¼ tsp baking powder
½ cup milk
1 ½ cups grated cheddar cheese
2 Tbsp cold butter, diced
½ tsp dried rosemary, chili flakes, or black pepper (optional for flavor)

DIRECTIONS:
1) Preheat oven to 375 F. Line a baking sheet with parchment paper.
2) Add all ingredients into a food processor and blend for 15-20 seconds until dough forms. Refrigerate dough ball for 5-10 minutes to reduce stickiness.
3) Dust a piece of parchment paper with flour. Place chilled dough ball onto parchment. Cover with another piece of parchment. Roll out until ¼ inch thickness. Cut dough into crackers by using cookie cutters or by safely using a knife. Re-roll and cut remaining dough until completed.
4) Bake 12-15 minutes or until crackers are golden. Cool on a wire rack and enjoy!

MEALS
BUTTERNUT SQUASH MAC AND CHEESE

Prep Time: 5 minutes

Cook Time: 20 minutes

Makes: 4 servings

INGREDIENTS:
1.5 cups peeled and cubed butternut squash (or 1.5 cups canned butternut squash puree for ease)
1/2 cup milk of choice
1 cup grated cheese (such as cheddar, mozzarella, jack, or a mix)
1 Tbsp butter or coconut oil
¼ tsp salt
8 ounces of dry pasta noodles (use a whole wheat or bean-based pasta for extra protein)
¼ cup panko breadcrumbs (optional)

DIRECTIONS:
1) Bring a large pot of water to a boil.
2) If using fresh butternut squash, add to boiling water and cook for about 10 minutes or until soft. Using a large slotted spoon, remove the butternut squash and place into a blender. Keep the water in the pot (you'll cook your noodles in here). Add the milk, cheese, and butter to the blender and puree until smooth without lumps.
3) Bring water back to a boil and cook pasta according to package instructions. Drain and rinse. Return pasta to the pot and pour over the cheesy squash sauce. Mix well.
4) Optional: Transfer the mac and cheese to a baking dish and top with panko breadcrumbs. Broil for 1-2 minutes until the panko turns golden brown.

CLASSIC MAC AND CHEESE

Prep Time:
5 minutes

Cook Time:
20 minutes

Makes:
4 servings

INGREDIENTS:
8 ounces of dry pasta noodles (use a whole wheat
or bean-based pasta for extra protein)
2 Tbsp unsalted butter
2 Tbsp all-purpose flour
1 ¼ cups milk of choice
1 cup grated cheese (such as cheddar, mozzarella, jack, or a mix)
¼ tsp salt
¼ cup panko breadcrumbs (optional)

DIRECTIONS:
1) Preheat oven to 400 F. Bring a large pot of water to a boil.
2) Cook pasta according to package instructions. Drain and rinse. Set aside.
3) Make a roux: melt butter in a saucepan over medium heat. Evenly sprinkle flour over the top and whisk to form a smooth paste. Whisk for a minute or two until fragrant. Slowly add the milk into the roux while whisking. It will get clumpy before it turns smooth. Keep adding the milk slowly and whisk until it finally turns into a sauce. Cook for another 5 minutes or until it starts to thicken. Add extra milk if it gets too thick.
4) Remove from heat and stir in the cheese and salt. Mix the sauce into the pasta.
5) Optional: Transfer the mac and cheese to a baking dish and top with panko breadcrumbs. Broil for 1-2 minutes until the panko turns golden brown.

FAMILY STYLE RAINBOW TACOS

Prep Time:
10 minutes

Cook Time:
15 minutes

Makes:
As many as you'd like

INGREDIENTS:

Tortillas: soft or hard shell
Protein Ideas: beans, grilled shrimp, fresh fish, shredded chicken, lean ground beef, veggie meatless grounds
Rainbow Topping Ideas:
Green: lettuce, spinach, green peppers, broccoli, cucumber, zucchini, cilantro, avocado
Yellow: yellow peppers, yellow tomatoes, yellow zucchini, pineapple
Orange: orange peppers, orange tomatoes, carrots, sweet potato
Red: peppers, tomatoes, salsa, red onion
Purple: purple cabbage, purple potatoes, purple carrots
Other delicious toppings: tasty tomato salsa, creamy avocado sauce, hot sauce, sour cream or Greek yogurt, cheese, olives, lime

DIRECTIONS:

1) Prepare ingredients together as a family. Place each ingredient in a separate bowl.
2) Everyone gets to make their own rainbow tacos! Use whatever toppings you like!

EGG ROLL BOWL

Prep Time: 15 minutes

Cook Time: 15 minutes

Makes: 4 servings

INGREDIENTS:
2 cups dry rice or 4 cups of riced cauliflower
2 Tbsp sesame oil
1 medium onion
1 clove garlic
1-pound of protein, your choice (firm tofu, or ground chicken, turkey, or pork)
2 cups shredded cabbage
1 Tbsp chili sauce/paste
1 Tbsp low sodium soy sauce or shoyu
1 Tbsp rice vinegar
Salt and pepper to taste

DIRECTIONS:
1) If using white or brown rice, cook according to package instructions.
2) Shred / thinly slice cabbage, chop onion, and mince garlic.
3) Heat sesame oil in a large non-stick skillet over medium-high heat. Add the onion and garlic. Cook until translucent and soft, about 3-5 minutes. Add your protein and cook until cooked through, about 5-8 minutes.
4) Add cabbage, soy sauce or shoyu, rice vinegar, and chili sauce. Stir fry until cabbage begins to soften.
5) If using cauliflower rice, prepare according to package instructions.
6) Serve your egg roll mixture over your rice or cauliflower rice.

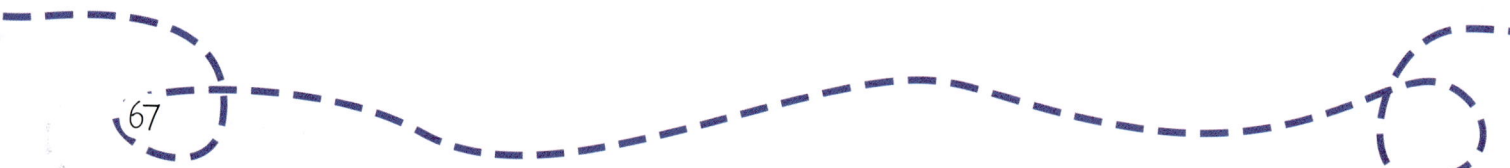

BAKED CHICKEN (OR TOFU) TENDERS

Prep Time: 10 minutes

Cook Time: 15-18 minutes

Makes: 4-6 servings

INGREDIENTS:
1-pound of chicken tenders or firm tofu
1 cup panko breadcrumbs
¼ tsp salt
2 eggs
1/3 cup all-purpose flour

DIRECTIONS:
1) Preheat oven to 425 F. Place a wire rack on a baking sheet. Grease the rack with vegetable oil or nonstick spray.
2) If using tofu, remove from package and wrap with a towel. Top with a plate and let sit for at least 15 minutes to remove extra liquid. Cut into strips, cubes, or triangles.
3) Whisk eggs in a one shallow dish. In another shallow dish, add the panko bread crumbs and salt. In a third shallow dish, add the flour.
4) Take one tender at a time and dunk completely in flour, then egg, then panko. Place on the prepared rack. Continue to do this until all of the chicken or tofu is coated. Spray lightly with nonstick spray.
5) Bake for 15-18 minutes or until cooked thoroughly. Serve warm with your favorite dipping sauce!

MELTY QUESADILLAS WITH SPINACH

Prep Time: 10 minutes

Cook Time: 10 minutes

Makes: 4 quesadillas

INGREDIENTS:
8 corn or small flour tortillas
1 cup shredded cheddar cheese
1 Tbsp cream cheese
3 cups fresh spinach
¼ tsp chili powder

DIRECTIONS:
1) Place cheese, cream cheese, spinach, and chili powder into a food processor and blend until smooth. If you don't have a food processor, chop spinach into small pieces and mix with other ingredients in a bowl.
2) Spoon and spread spinach cheese mixture onto 4 tortillas. Top each with a second tortilla.
3) Heat a non-stick pan over medium heat. Lightly grease with vegetable oil if you want golden browned tortillas (optional). Cook each quesadilla for 2-3 minutes on each side or until golden and insides are warm.

SIMPLE PEANUT NOODLES

Prep Time:
5 minutes

Cook Time:
10 minutes

Makes:
4 servings

INGREDIENTS:
8 ounces dry rice noodles
1/2 carrot
½ cup shelled edamame
1 green onion stalk
2 Tbsp cup low sodium soy sauce or shoyu
1 Tbsp lime juice
1 tsp sesame oil
2 Tbsp unsalted peanut butter (non-hydrogenated)
1 tsp honey
Optional toppings: peanuts, fresh cilantro, lime, chili sauce/paste

DIRECTIONS:
1) Prepare your ingredients. Chop the carrots and green onions.
2) Cook rice noodles according to package instructions. Drain and do not rinse.
3) Make the sauce. Mix the soy sauce, lime juice, sesame oil, peanut butter, honey, and garlic in a bowl with a whisk or fork until combined.
4) Add your chopped carrots, onions, edamame, and sauce into the pot with the noodles. Mix evenly.
5) Serve warm or cold with your favorite toppings.

SPAGHETTI SQUASH ALFREDO

Prep Time: 10 minutes

Cook Time: 1 hour 30 minutes

Makes: 2-4 servings

INGREDIENTS:
1 medium spaghetti squash
1 Tbsp butter
2 Tbsp all-purpose flour
2 cloves garlic
1 cup milk of choice
1 Tbsp cream cheese
1 cup freshly grated parmesan cheese, save some for topping
Salt and pepper to taste
Fresh basil to top

DIRECTIONS:
1) Preheat oven to 350 F.
2) Cut spaghetti squash in half and scoop out the seeds. Place cut side down on a rimmed baking sheet with a splash of water. Bake for 45 minutes - 1 hour, or until tender. Remove from oven and cool for 10 minutes.
3) Use a fork to scrape the inside of the squash into spaghetti.
4) Make the sauce by melting the butter in a small pot over low-medium heat. Add garlic and cook for 1-2 minutes. Add flour and whisk in for 1 minute. Add milk and whisk until smooth. Add the cream cheese, parmesan, and salt and pepper. Stir until melted.
5) Spoon sauce onto each spaghetti squash half. Mix gently and top with extra parmesan cheese. Broil for 1-2 minutes or until golden. Top with fresh basil and enjoy!

VEGGIE TAQUITOS

Prep Time: 15 minutes   Cook Time: 20 minutes   Makes: 12 taquitos

INGREDIENTS:
1 tsp vegetable oil such as olive, avocado, or coconut oil
1 red, yellow, or orange bell pepper
½ bunch cilantro, chopped
1/3 cup cream cheese, softened
¼ cup favorite salsa
1 – 15 ounce can black beans
Juice of 1 lime
½ tsp cumin
12 small flour tortillas

DIRECTIONS:
1) Preheat oven to 425 F.
2) Dice bell pepper, drain and rinse black beans.
3) Heat oil in a non-stick pan over medium-high heat. Cook bell pepper for 2-3 minutes.
4) Add beans, softened cream cheese, salsa, cumin, and lime juice to pan. Stir and heat until warmed, making sure to lightly mash the beans into the mixture. Turn heat off and add chopped cilantro.
5) Spoon about 2 Tbsp mixture onto each tortilla. Wrap and place seam side down on baking sheet and spray or lightly brush top of taquitos with oil.
6) Bake for 15 minutes or until golden. Allow to cool for a few minutes before serving.

HAWAIIAN FRIED RICE

Prep Time: 10 minutes

Cook Time: 45 minutes (includes rice)

Makes: 4-6 servings

INGREDIENTS:
1.5 cups dry rice (white or brown)
2 cloves garlic
¼ cup pineapple or orange juice
1/3 cup low sodium soy sauce or shoyu
2 Tbsp honey
1 Tbsp sesame oil
1 Tbsp vegetable oil such as avocado or coconut oil
2 cups vegetables (such as onion, carrots, and peas)
1 cup pineapple chunks (fresh, frozen, or canned)
3 eggs
Optional Toppings: 2 green onion stalks, cashew nuts, and fresh cilantro

DIRECTIONS:
1) Cook rice according to package instructions
2) Make the sauce. Mince garlic and place into a medium sized bowl. Add juice, soy sauce or shoyu, honey, and sesame oil. Mix well.
3) Heat vegetable oil in a large pan over medium-high heat. Add the vegetables and pineapple to the pan. Cook for about 5 minutes. Turn heat down to low-medium.
4) Make a space in the center of the pan and add the eggs. Stir to scramble the eggs.
5) Add cooked rice and sauce to pan. Mix well. Serve with your favorite toppings!

PEANUT BUTTER CURRY

Prep Time: 5 minutes   Cook Time: 10 minutes   Makes: 3-4 servings

INGREDIENTS:
1 tsp vegetable oil (such as coconut, avocado, or olive oil)
1 clove garlic
¾ cup water
¼ cup peanut butter (non-hydrogenated)
Juice of 1 lime
1 ½ Tbsp maple syrup (or honey)
½ tsp curry powder
1 – 15 ounce can of garbanzo beans, drained and rinsed
Salt and pepper to taste
Optional toppings: fresh cilantro, lime juice, hot sauce

DIRECTIONS:
1) In a sauce pot over medium heat, heat the oil and then add the minced garlic. Cook for 1 minute.
2) Add the water, peanut butter, lime juice, maple syrup, and curry powder. Stir often until it begins to boil. Lower heat and continue to stir until sauce is thick.
3) Add the garbanzo beans and stir. Cook on low heat for 3-5 more minutes. Add salt and pepper to taste (you may not need any salt if your peanut butter is salted).
4) Remove from heat and serve with your favorite toppings.

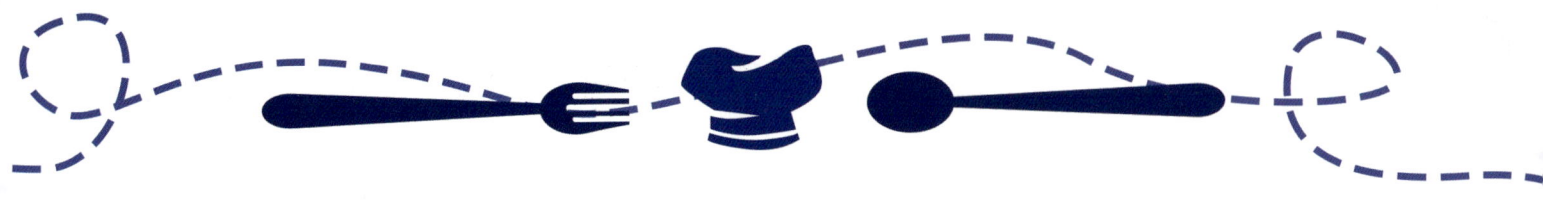

LEMON BUTTER PASTA

Prep Time: 5 minutes

Cook Time: 10 minutes

Makes: 4-6 servings

INGREDIENTS:
1-pound of dry spaghetti (try a whole wheat or bean-based pasta for extra nutritional value)
1 cup roughly chopped walnuts, pine nuts, or pistachios
2 Tbsp butter
2 Tbsp olive oil
½ tsp salt
2 small lemons, zested and juiced
Optional Toppings: freshly grated parmesan cheese, black pepper, and fresh parsley

DIRECTIONS:
1) Bring a large pot of water to a boil. Cook pasta according to package instructions.
2) Toast nuts in a small pan over medium heat for 5 minutes or until fragrant and beginning to turn golden brown. Remove from heat.
3) Reserve ½ cup of the pasta cooking water. Drain pasta and return back to pot. Stir in the butter, oil, salt, toasted nuts, lemon juice, and lemon zest. Add pasta water as needed to thin sauce.
4) Serve with your favorite toppings.

DESSERTS
COCONUT SWEET RICE WITH MANGO

Prep Time: minutes

Cook Time: minutes

Makes: 2 servings

INGREDIENTS:
1 cup cooked white or brown rice
1/2 cup coconut milk
1/2 tsp vanilla extract
1 Tbsp honey or maple syrup
1 cup fresh or frozen mango (thawed) for topping

DIRECTIONS:
1) Heat rice, coconut milk, vanilla extract, and honey or maple syrup in a sauce pan over medium heat for 8-10 minutes. Stir often.
2) Place in bowls and let cool. Chop mango and top pudding. Serve chilled or at room temperature.

CHOCOLATE PUDDING

Prep Time: 5 minutes

Makes: 3-4 servings

INGREDIENTS:
1 medium ripe avocado
½ cup Greek yogurt
2 Tbsp unsweetened cocoa powder
2 Tbsp maple syrup
1 tsp vanilla extract

DIRECTIONS:
1) Scoop out the avocado flesh. Discard the pit and skins.
2) Add all ingredients to a blender and blend until combined. Stop and scrape down the sides of the blender as needed to move pudding closer to blender blade.

FROZEN BANANA POPS

Prep Time:
10 minutes

Makes:
6 pops

INGREDIENTS:
6 popsicle sticks
2 bananas
¾ cup semi-sweet chocolate chips
Optional toppings: peanuts, coconut flakes, flax seed, chia seeds

DIRECTIONS:
1) Line a baking sheet or large plate with parchment paper. Cut each banana into 3 equal pieces and gently insert popsicle sticks into the center to each piece like a popsicle.
2) Melt the chocolate chips in a microwave safe bowl and melt in the microwave, stirring every 30 seconds. Chop nuts into small pieces. Dip the banana pops in the melted chocolate. Top with desired toppings. Toppings can be used without chocolate too.
3) Place banana pops onto the baking sheet or plate. Freeze for at least 2 hours before enjoying!

RAINBOW FRUIT KABOBS WITH HEALTHY CAKE BATTER DIP

Prep Time: 10 minutes

Makes: 1 cup batter and as many kabobs as you'd like!

INGREDIENTS:
Bamboo skewer sticks
Assortment of fruit in all colors of the rainbow (banana, oranges, berries, kiwis, melon)
1 cup cottage cheese
½ tsp vanilla extract
1 Tbsp honey or pure maple syrup
2 Tbsp milk of choice (unsweetened vanilla almond milk works well)
2 Tbsp dry oats or graham cracker crumbs
Optional: rainbow sprinkles for serving

DIRECTIONS:
1) Cut fruit into ½ inch thick slices. You can also use a melon baller for melon.
2) Place fruit pieces onto skewer in a rainbow pattern.
3) Blend dry oats or graham crackers in a blender until flour consistency. Add the rest of the cake batter dip ingredients to the blender and puree until smooth with no lumps.
4) Serve cake batter dip in a bowl and top with sprinkles if desired. Dip fruit kabobs in batter for a healthy treat!

WATERMELON POPSICLES

Prep Time:
10 minutes

Makes:
6-8 popsicles

INGREDIENTS:
2 cups watermelon slices, black seeds removed
1 cup coconut water
1 Tbsp lemon or lime juice
1 Tbsp honey or maple syrup

DIRECTIONS:
1) Blend all of your ingredients together in a blender.
2) Pour your popsicle mixture into popsicle molds, ice cube trays, or paper cups. Insert the popsicle sticks.
3) Freeze for at least 6 hours for a frozen treat!

CARROT CAKE COOKIES

Prep Time: 20 minutes

Cook Time: 15-18 minutes

Makes: 12 cookies

INGREDIENTS:
1 cup quick-cooking oats
1 cup all-purpose flour (or whole wheat)
1 tsp baking powder
1 tsp cinnamon
½ tsp nutmeg
½ tsp salt
1 ½ cup grated carrot
1 cup chopped nuts of choice
½ cup raisins (regular or golden)
½ cup honey or pure maple syrup
½ cup coconut oil, melted

DIRECTIONS:
1) Preheat oven to 375 F. Line baking sheets with parchment paper.
2) In a large bowl, mix the oats, flour, cinnamon, nutmeg, baking powder, and salt. Add the carrots, nuts, and raisins. Stir until well combined.
3) In a separate bowl, mix the honey or maple syrup, and coconut oil. Pour the wet ingredients into the dry. Stir until combined.
4) Use hands to shape dough into cookies and flatten slightly.
5) Bake for 15-18 minutes, or until beginning to golden. If baking more than one pan at a time, rotate pans halfway through baking. Let cookies cool on baking sheet for a few minutes before moving to a wire rack to cool completely.

DRINKS
ELECTROLYTE BUZZ

Prep Time: 5 minutes

Makes: 3-4 servings

INGREDIENTS:
½ cup frozen fruit
1 Tbsp honey
¼ tsp salt
3 cups coconut water

DIRECTIONS:
Blend all of the ingredients in a blender until liquid. Drink on a hot day!

SO BERRY DELICIOUS SUN TEA

Prep Time: 10 minutes

Sun Time: 6 hours

Makes: 3-4 servings

INGREDIENTS:
3 cups water
3 fruity tea bags (strawberry, raspberry, peach, etc.)
½ cup apple juice
3-5 strawberries (or other fresh fruit of choice)
1 Tbsp honey
Ice cubes and fresh mint to serve

DIRECTIONS:
1) Pour water into a large mason jar or pitcher. Add tea bags and close the top with a lid, foil, or cloth with a rubber band. Place in the sun for at least 6 hours.
2) Remove tea bags. Add sliced strawberries, apple juice, and honey.
3) Serve over ice cubes and with a fresh sprig of mint

HORCHATA

Prep Time:
2 hours 20 minutes

Makes:
4 cups

INGREDIENTS:
¾ cup long grain white rice
5 cups water (divided)
½ cup pitted dates (or sub ¼ cup honey or pure maple syrup)
1 ½ tsp vanilla extract
½ tsp ground cinnamon

DIRECTIONS:
1) Heat 2 cups of water until hot (not boiling). Soak rice for 2 hours in hot water until beginning to soften but still pretty raw.
2) Drain rice and add to blender with 3 cups of water, sweetener (dates, honey, or maple syrup), vanilla extract, and cinnamon. Cover the lid of your blender with a towel in case it splashes. Blend for 1 minute until well combined.
3) Strain the mixture into a bowl or pitcher using a cheesecloth, nut milk bag, clean t-shirt, or even clean panty hose. Squeeze out all of the liquid.
4) Serve over ice with a sprinkle of cinnamon and enjoy!

HOT COCOA

Prep Time:
2 minutes

Cook Time:
5 minutes

Makes:
2 cups

INGREDIENTS:
2 cups of milk or non-dairy milk of choice
2 Tbsp unsweetened cocoa powder
2 Tbsp honey or pure maple syrup
½ tsp vanilla extract
Tiny pinch salt

DIRECTIONS:
1) Heat milk in a small saucepan of low-medium heat. Once warm, whisk in cocoa powder, honey or maple syrup, vanilla extract, and tiny pinch of salt.
2) Serve warm!

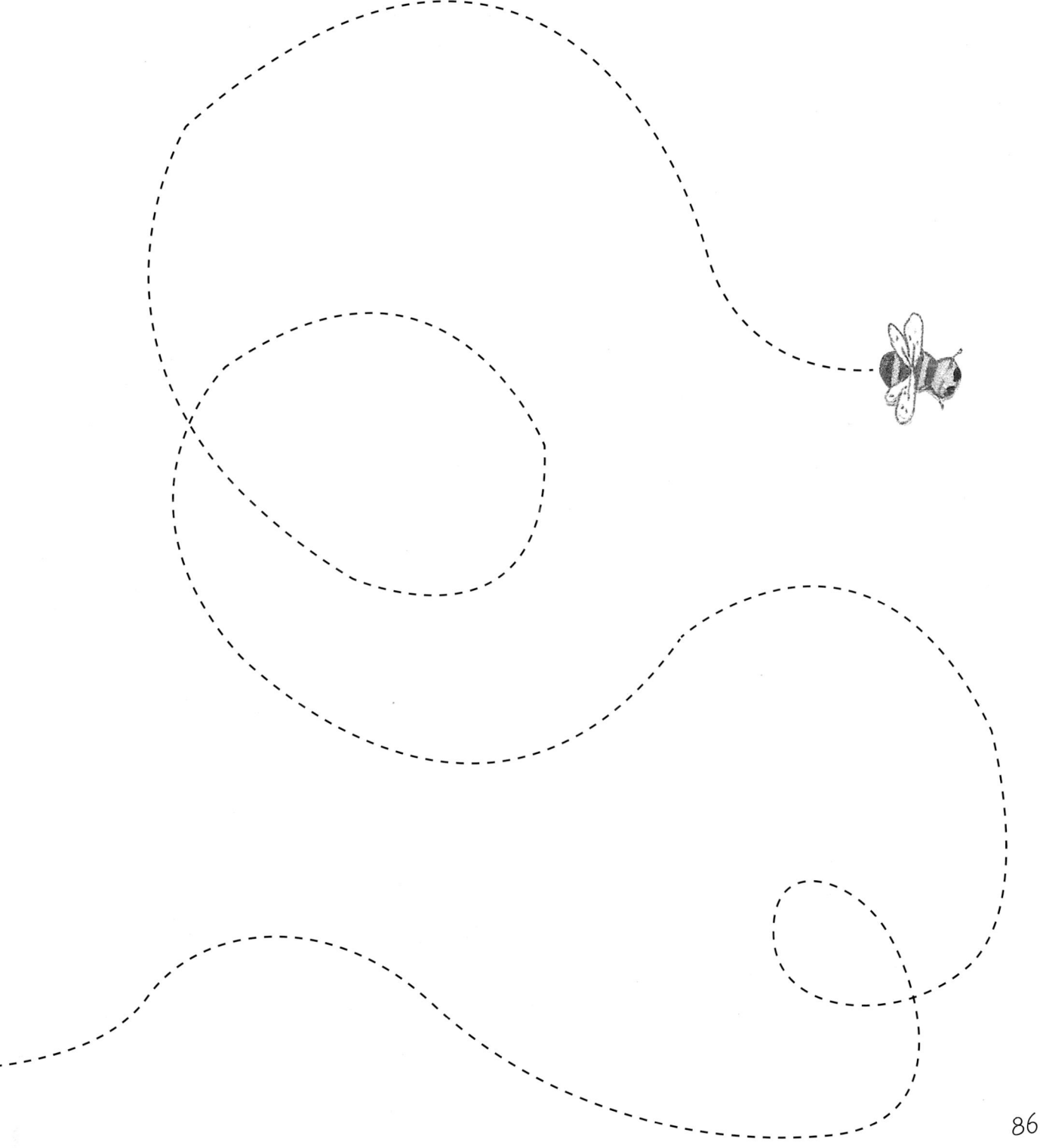

HOW TO MAKE A SMOOTHIE

Smoothies are a tasty frozen treat on a hot day! A good smoothie can satisfy your thirst and give you long-lasting energy. Each food group has its own special powers – they help you play hard, grow muscles, and think smart. Pick ingredients from each group!

FRUITS: berries, banana, mango, apples, peaches, watermelon, kiwi, and pineapple

VEGGIES: zucchini, cauliflower, carrots, avocado, pumpkin, edamame, and spinach

PROTEIN: yogurt, nut butters, seeds, tofu, and cottage cheese

LIQUIDS: water, ice, your favorite milk, coconut water, a squeeze of lemon or lime, a splash of fruit juice, vegetable juice

FUN STUFF: graham crackers, oatmeal, chocolate, vanilla, sprinkles

SMOOTHIES – 4 WAYS

Prep Time: 5 minutes

Each Recipe Makes: 2 smoothies

DIRECTIONS:
It's easy! Add all of the ingredients to a blender and blend until smooth. Poor into cups.

ORANGE SUNRISE

INGREDIENTS:
1 large frozen banana
6 baby carrots
½ cup vanilla Greek yogurt
½ cup orange juice
and ½ cup water

VERY VANILLA

INGREDIENTS:
1 frozen banana
1 cup shelled frozen edamame
1 Tbsp almond butter
½ tsp vanilla extract
1 cup milk or non-dairy milk of choice

CHOCOLATE MONKEY

INGREDIENTS:
2 frozen bananas
¼ cup peanut butter (non-hydrogenated)
2 Tbsp unsweetened cocoa powder
½ tsp vanilla extract (optional)
1 cup milk or non-dairy milk of choice

STRAWBERRY CAKE SHAKE

INGREDIENTS:
1 frozen banana
1 cup strawberries
½ cup cottage cheese
1 cup milk or non-dairy milk or choice
Top with a pinch of sprinkles

My Recipes

My Recipes

My Recipes

My Recipes

My Recipes

My Recipes

TIPS ON FIRST FOODS FOR BABIES

INTRODUCING SOLID FOODS

Babies are ready to be introduced to solid foods at 4-6 months of age once they can demonstrate:

- Ability to sit with support
- Good head and neck control
- Transitioning from using their sucking reflex to swallowing. Your baby does not push a spoon out with their tongue when it is placed into their mouth.
- Has an interest about solid foods

Ask your pediatrician if you have any questions about their readiness. Here is some helpful guidance for once you decide to introduce solid foods:

- Offering new foods to your baby is all about exposing them to new flavors and textures! Don't fret if they seem to eat very little at first. It can take several weeks for them to begin mastering the art of swallowing food. Continue to offer breast milk or formula while introducing solid foods.
- Babies don't need water when they are exclusively on breast milk and/or formula. Giving water risks displacing their appetite for nutrient rich breast milk and/or formula. You can start offering sips of water when you introduce solid foods.
- Let you baby guide feeding. Are they acting interested in food? Are they acting full? It's important to pay attention to their cues. They will tell you when they are full.
- Young babies don't need 3 solid food meals a day. You can start working towards 3 meals a day as they get older at 9-11 months.
- Choose foods that will be easy for your baby to pick up to practice feeding themselves. Offering a baby spoon with meals lets them practice from the get go! Anticipate messes - they are a part of learning!
- Do not give honey to children under the age of one. Honey can cause infant botulism.

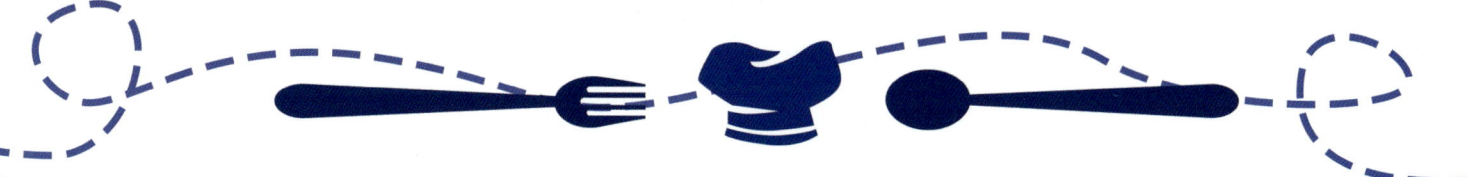

OFFER YOUR BABY IRON-RICH FOODS FIRST!

Breast milk and formula is high in iron, an important mineral that helps with brain development and blood circulation. At around 6 months, both baby and mom's iron stores start to deplete and breast milk becomes less iron rich. That's why introducing high iron foods are important! There are two types of iron: heme iron (from meat) and non-heme iron (from plant sources). Pair non-heme sources of iron with a vitamin C rich food to boost absorption.

Heme Iron Sources	Non-Heme Iron Sources	Vitamin C Sources
beef, pork, chicken, eggs, salmon, tuna	leafy greens, prunes, oats, brown rice, quinoa, beans, soybeans, blackstrap molasses, mushrooms and chia seeds	tomatoes, bell peppers, citrus fruits including lemon and lime juice, strawberries, kiwi, pineapple

INTRODUCING POTENTIAL FOOD ALLERGENS

The top 8 allergens are: milk, eggs, fish, shellfish, tree nuts, peanuts, wheat, and soybean

There is increasing evidence that introducing the top 8 food allergens as early as 4-6 months of age, rather than waiting to introduce, can reduce the risk and even help prevent the development of true food allergies.[2-5] Introduce these foods one at a time. This will help you quickly identify whether a food is causing a reaction such as hives, swelling, redness, and a rash. Consult with your pediatrician on introducing allergens to high risk babies, such as if there is a family history of food allergies, severe eczema, asthma, and other diagnosed food allergies.

CHOKING HAZARDS FOR BABIES & CHILDREN UNDER 4

Your baby has a higher chance for choking if they are distracted during eating, or if they are moving while eating. Create a calm eating environment! Round and circular foods pose the highest risk. Here is a list of top hazards to avoid, and ways to modify these foods to make them safer:

Choking Hazard!	Instead Try This!
Chunks of raw vegetables	Grate, thinly slice, or make 'noodles' with them
Cherry tomatoes and grapes	Quarter lengthwise
Nuts, seeds, or a spoonful of nut butter	Smooth nut and seed butters thinly spread
Dried fruit	Fresh or pureed fruit
Hotdogs	Quarter lengthwise, then cut into bite size

* Don't offer popcorn, hard candies, or gum under the age of 4

GROWING LIFELONG HEALTHY EATERS

Learning to try new foods is a part of growing up, yet it can often lead to mealtime meltdowns! This section is to support parents with evidenced-based approaches to creating stress-free family meals and growing lifelong healthy eaters.

THE DIVISION OF RESPONSIBILITY

The Division of Responsibility is a framework developed by Ellyn Satter, child nutrition expert and psychotherapist.[1] These guiding principles are rooted in boundaries and establish positive feeding practices to help our children build a lifelong healthy relationship with food.

In the Division of Responsibility, parents and children each have their own jobs when it comes to eating:

- Parents decide what foods to offer, when, and where
- Children decide what they want to eat from the offered foods, and how much

Here are some tips to put this into practice:

Start with giving your child the love and comfort of knowing they will have regular and routine meals and snacks to reduce their anxiety. Let the focus of mealtime be spending enjoyable time together as a family.

Stay in your lane! Your job as a parent is to pick what foods will be served for snacks and meals, when you will offer them, and where. Children are free to refuse these foods, eat seconds, be full when they say they are, and learn to recognize that not every snack or meal is going to be their favorite.

Children have excellent hunger and fullness cues. Their eating will ebb and flow; evidence supports that it is natural for children to have varied eating. Some days you may wonder how they eat so little, and other days they may eat what seems like their total nutrition needs for the week! This is based on their natural hunger and fullness cues and is perfectly normal. Parents can negatively interfere in a number of ways: being too restrictive with their eating can make children become fixated on food; letting them have full access to the refrigerator or pantry at any time can decrease willingness to try new foods; and making them "clean their plate" overrides their ability to eat mindfully and stop when they are full.

It is okay for children to be hesitant about new foods. A new food can be difficult to master; from texture, to smell, to taste, it can take many exposures before a child is comfortable with trying it. That is okay! Sooner or later kids will take interest in these foods, and they are more likely to do so when there is no pressure. Avoid pressure talk such as, "you need to eat your broccoli before you can leave the table". Children feel a sense of autonomy and pride when they choose to eat a new food and master it on their own. That is a far superior lesson than getting them to cheerlessly down a mouthful of vegetables at dinner. The more pressure you put on your child to eat a certain food, the more you are sending a message that "this food must not be good if my parents are trying to force me to eat it". Rather, set a good example with your own eating and stay in your lane with the Division of Responsibility. It is your child's job to choose when they will try new foods.

Don't short order cook. Instead, focus on making sure there are 1-2 foods you know are acceptable to your child with each meal. Also, include a new food or one they have not mastered yet to build exposure. This will reduce your anxiety that they won't have anything to eat, and it will gently teach them that not all meals will be their favorite.

FAMILY STYLE MEALS

Family style meals are a fantastic way for everyone to construct their own plate, have plenty of opportunities to try different ingredients, and teach sharing to children. Here are some considerations:

Try allowing your child to serve them self. This not only will build dexterity but will give your child feelings of accomplishment.

When you allow your child to serve them self or with your help, avoid insisting that every food must be tried. Children are more likely to try something if they take an active role in the decision making.

Allow them to have seconds if they are still hungry.

Keep in mind that kids won't always eat every food group at each meal. Don't put pressure on them to do so. You may find they don't take a vegetable at first, but later in the meal they want to try it.

Avoid the "no thank you bite". This goes against the Division of Responsibility and gives children unnecessary anxiety related to eating. The goal is to establish a lifelong healthy relationship with food; forcing food goes against that. See below on how you can positively use your language to encourage trying a new food.

Be a good role model. Your child will observe that you have a diverse diet and will innately want to work their way up to eating a large variety of foods like you.

Most importantly, enjoy each other's company! Children often eat more adventurously when they are relaxed.

BUILDING FAMILIARITY WITH NEW FOODS

The most important takeaway in building familiarity with new foods is to offer, offer, offer! By increasing a child's willingness to try new foods, you are helping to broaden their horizons.

Recognize that children learn the world around them through using their 5 senses: sight, sound, smell, taste, and touch. Learning a new food is no different. Encourage them to use their 5 senses to become familiar with new foods. Again, avoid pressure talk. If your child doesn't want to taste it, that is fine! Touching, smelling, and talking about it is all progress.

Keep offering a food they are unsure about in new ways. If they didn't like steamed carrots, what about carrot fries, carrot soup, or a carrot smoothie? The same goes for flavor profiles. How about an Indian food style pizza, or their favorite pasta noodle with a new kind of sauce?

Get them involved in the decision making. Let them choose the fruits and vegetables when grocery shopping. What vegetables would they like to add in the soup, stir fry, or smoothie?

Read your child books about food and where it comes from, such as this alphabet cookbook! Reading fun books with illustrations is a low-stress way for your child to become comfortable and inquisitive about new fruits and vegetables.

Plant a garden together. This could be as simple as a kitchen windowsill herb garden or as wondrous as a backyard vegetable garden with fruit trees. Letting your child see how food grows and become invested in the process can increase their willingness to want to try the food. However, remember they still have a choice. Offer to make food together using your garden ingredients. If they don't want to taste it, be a good example and eat it yourself! Let them see the joy it brought you to grow this food and make a meal together.

ADJUSTING OUR THOUGHTS AND WORDS

Teaching your child to think positively about food:

Rather than pressuring your child to try a new food, you can provide gentle encouragement by saying, "There are many foods that you love. Imagine if you had never tried them before (cookies, mac and cheese)? Without trying, you could be missing out on a delicious food". If they decline trying it let them know it's okay and they will have an opportunity to again.

If your child tries a food and gives a big "yuck!", take it as an opportunity to teach about how to politely say they don't like it. Explain that someone worked hard to grow this food, and that many people enjoy it. Saying yuck could be hurtful. Teach them that it is more respectful to say, "that's not my favorite", or a simple "no thank you".

Explore with your child how there are many different varieties of fruits and vegetables, and just because you didn't like one doesn't mean you won't like another. For example, if when trying apples your child says the green one is too sour, you can say, "Wow, that one was really sour. I thought it would be sweet! Let's try another kind of apple and see if it will be sweeter".

Adjusting our own thoughts as adults:

Work on trusting your child's hunger and fullness cues. You did your job if you served a variety of foods at a meal. Now approach their eating with curiosity such as thinking, "I wonder what they are going to try tonight". If they don't put much on their plate, practice thinking, "If my child isn't eating much tonight, then they must not be hungry." Making comments to your child about how picky they are takes away their pride and autonomy with eating.

Rather than stress on your child's nutritional intake over a day, reflect on their intake over a week or a month. Remember that a child's intakes will go up and down with their hunger and fullness cues, and that varied intake is normal. You can use this information in planning your upcoming meals. For instance, if they were short on a food group yesterday, you can keep trying to offer this food group at other meals.

WAYS OF USING THE ALPHABET COOKBOOK, AND YOUR IMAGINATION AS A LEARNING TOOL FOR ALL AGES!

READING AND VOCABULARY ACTIVITIES

You can practice alphabet skills in many ways for different levels of learning. Beginning with just reading as a picture book to young children and pointing to the letters. Advancing to reading and pointing to each word as you read to help create words known by sight. Have the child repeat the names of the letters, and the sound the letter makes to practice pronunciation. A child will be able to read first the letters, then some words, and eventually the book.

Older children can read the book to younger children and help them to learn the alphabet. They can also practice writing the letters, numbers and words they now recognize. Flash cards (making them can be a fun craft project!) are a great way to practice sight recognition of letters, words or numbers.

Use visual aids (the actual items or pictures) to create activities that teach the words in the book. For example, put an apple, a piece of bread and a cookie on a plate. Younger children can point to the item when asked "Where is the _____?"

As they get older, they can write the name of the item you point to, or match them to the written words. These are just two examples, but there are endless ways of using visual aids to teach, and you can use the pictures in the book if no real items are available.

Use the colors found in the pictures of the book and the numbers on the word list to practice learning colors and numbers.

Examples of all the primary (red, blue and yellow) and secondary (orange, green and purple) along with black, white and brown are represented on the cover and in many of the pictures of the book. Start with fewer numbers for younger children (1-10), and work up to the number 100 with older children. Early number practice can be as simple as counting items in the pictures. Math skills can be taught using equivalents and recipes being halved or doubled for older children.

Think of different foods, or other words that start with each letter with your child.

Older children can be shown grammar points in the text, examples of when to use periods, commas, question marks and quotation marks can be discussed. Also, how words become plural can be a lesson.

Point out the lower case and capital versions of the letters.

Point out rhyming words in the text and try to think of other words that rhyme together.

Create simple sentences, for example - I like _____. or This is a _____. Have the child fill in the blank with word list words.

Help the child write down one of their favorite recipes on the pages provided in the book.

HEALTHY FOOD ACTIVITIES

Always use the time you are making a recipe with a child to teach them kitchen safety! The importance of being supervised, and being safe around stovetops, ovens, knives, etc. There are two pages in the book with some safety tips to go over before you start to cook.

See how many things younger children can point to in the kitchen when asked "Where is the_____?"

Older children can learn the different terms of cooking: simmer, boil, baste, steam, fry, etc. They can plan a menu and create a shopping list among other things.

Show children your spices, let them smell them and tell them where they come from and when you use them.

Show them herbs in the store or farmers market, let them smell them and imagine how to use them.

Use measuring spoons, cups and pots to teach measurements.

Plant some vegetables or herbs that are easy to grow in a pot with a child, and then let them use what they grow when cooking.

Investigate with your child why apple trees (and so much of our food) depends on bees.

Spend quality time together cooking, gardening, shopping, or going to the farmers market. Point out things the child will know from the book.

Go over the balanced plate information on page 35 in this book with your child and have a talk with them about how eating good will make them feel better, do better and be better!

REFERENCES

1. Satter E. Child of Mine: Feeding with Love and Good Sense. Palo Alto, CA: Bull Pub.; 2000.
2. Du Toit G, Roberts G, Sayre PH, et al. Randomized trial of peanut consumption in infants at risk for peanut allergy [published correction appears in N Engl J Med. 2016 Jul 28;375(4):398]. N Engl J Med. 2015;372(9):803-813. doi:10.1056/NEJMoa1414850
3. Du Toit G, Sayre PH, Roberts G, et al. Effect of Avoidance on Peanut Allergy after Early Peanut Consumption. N Engl J Med. 2016;374(15):1435-1443. doi:10.1056/NEJMoa1514209
4. Perkin MR, Logan K, Tseng A, et al. Randomized Trial of Introduction of Allergenic Foods in Breast-Fed Infants. N Engl J Med. 2016;374(18):1733-1743. doi:10.1056/NEJMoa1514210
5. Al-Saud B, Sigurdardóttir ST. Early Introduction of Egg and the Development of Egg Allergy in Children: A Systematic Review and Meta-Analysis. Int Arch Allergy Immunol. 2018;177(4):350-359. doi:10.1159/000492131